Helping
Our Animal Friends

Two boys are feeding their pet goldfish. As one boy watches, the other shakes just the right amount of food into the water.

by

Judith E. Rinard

Photographs by

Susan McElhinney

BOOKS FOR YOUNG EXPLORERS
NATIONAL GEOGRAPHIC SOCIETY

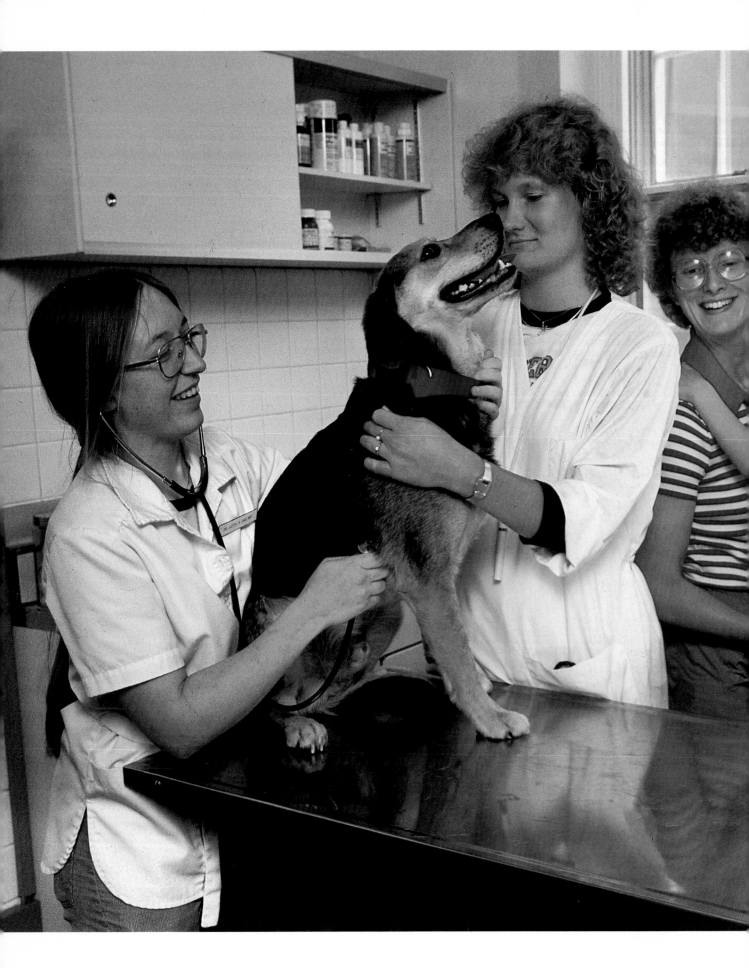

A new family pet is getting a checkup from a veterinarian. The animal doctor listens to the dog's heart. She wants to make sure it is healthy and well. Next, she will check the eyes, ears, nose, and teeth.

Animals need help from their owners in many ways. They need good care, food, water, a home, and love. Getting checkups for your pet is one way you can help it. What else can you do? Let's see!

Animals need many kinds of care. Kristen made a warm bed from a box for her cat and four little kittens. The mother cat rests as her kittens nurse, safe in their cozy bed.
On a farm, Caroline runs with her pet lamb. Running gives him good exercise and helps keep him healthy.

Two ducks splash and paddle. To stay healthy, ducks need water for swimming. They clean themselves in the water. With their bills, they put their feathers in order. This is called preening.

All pets need to be fed. For a snack, Caroline and Elizabeth give their lamb milk from a bottle. Elizabeth keeps him still by holding his rope. The girls enjoy feeding their pet and playing with him in the grassy field.

A farm is a good place for lambs because they need a lot of open space. In the city, it is hard to keep farm animals like lambs as pets.

Whitney rests with his pet dog after school. The mixed
German shepherd is a big dog and needs a lot of exercise.
Whitney runs and plays with him outside each day.

To feed his pet, Whitney mixes canned dog food with dry
food. This makes a complete meal.
Once in a while, he adds an egg
as a special treat.

The healthy dog is a good friend.
He needs Whitney to care for him
every single day.

When it's cold and snowy, many animals have a hard time finding food. People often help them. Two finches crack open seeds at a bird feeder hung from a branch. On a feeder nailed to a tree, a squirrel nibbles corn. A farmer puts out hay for a cow and her calf.

You, too, can help your animal friends by putting out food. Birds love suet, a kind of fat, as well as many kinds of seeds. Squirrels eat nuts. A feeding place just for squirrels may help keep them away from bird feeders.

If you set out a feeder, remember to keep it filled all winter. The animals will depend on you for their food.

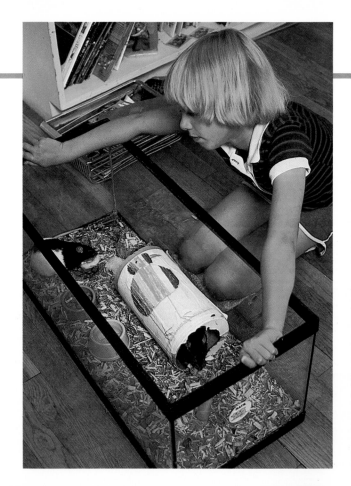

Small pet animals that live indoors
need a place of their own.
Do you have a small pet?

Sarah's pets are black-and-white
rats. One rat explores a cardboard
tube that Sarah put in the glass
cage. The two rats like to play and
hide. Sarah gives them fresh water
and rat food every day. Sometimes
they get carrots and greens, too.

Marcus cleans his parakeets' cage. Each day, he changes
the paper on the tray. He gives the parakeets fresh food and
water every day. The two birds keep each other company.

At school, Lisa can see little ducklings hatch from eggs. A box called an incubator has lightbulbs that keep the eggs warm.

Lisa and her class learned that eggs need to stay warm so baby birds can hatch. The school will find good homes for the ducklings.

Nick and Justin enjoy watching their goldfish. The plant and castle give the fish places to hide.

Holly takes her pony North Star for a swim in a pond.
On a hot summer day, the water helps the pony cool off.
It also gives him a rest. Horses enjoy swimming just as
you do. Water helps animals in many ways.

These children are giving their friend North Star a bath.
They scrub the pony gently with warm soapy water,
cleaning him from head to tail. Two girls carefully wash
his head. They talk to him quietly so he will stay calm.
To finish the job, the children will dry and brush him.

An English cocker spaniel named Foggy is getting
a warm sudsy bath. The bath helps get rid of fleas
and will make him smell good.

A teacher shows the children how to wash Foggy's
skin and coat. They will dry him quickly
with towels so he doesn't get cold.

Many children who live on farms
raise animals as projects for 4-H
clubs. One little girl learns
how to brush a sheep.

An older girl uses clippers to cut
her steer's hair. She is grooming it
for a show at a fair.
She raised the steer from a calf.

On the day of the fair, this girl finishes grooming her horse. She paints its hooves with a polish that makes them shiny. The polish helps keep the hooves from cracking and splitting. Many boys and girls learn about farm animals by joining clubs such as 4-H. The clubs teach grooming and other skills needed to care for animals.

A robin splashes in a birdbath. Birds need water all year. Bathing helps them get rid of dirt and bugs. Water running from a hose keeps a birdbath from freezing in winter.

If you have a birdbath, you can watch wild birds as they
come to bathe. Just be sure to keep fresh water in it. Place it
in the open, where cats cannot sneak up on the birds.

Sometimes wild animals need help from people
in special ways. This boy is helping a park ranger
feed meat to two orphan baby opossums.

At an animal shelter, two girls watch a tiny baby squirrel.
It had fallen from its nest and was helpless. Workers at the
shelter are caring for the squirrel. They will let it go when it is
grown. If you find a sick or injured animal, do not touch it.
Ask an adult to call an animal shelter or the Humane Society.

Who's the baby-sitter for this little deer? A goat!
A wildlife worker put the fawn with a nanny goat
to nurse. The fawn's own mother had died.
The worker is careful not to make a pet of the
fawn. When it is old enough to find its own
food, it will be set free to live in the wild.

What's for lunch? Screech owl babies eat fresh
meat. These orphan owls are being cared for at
a nature center. Owls in the wild catch mice and
insects. These young owls must learn to hunt on
their own before they are put back in the woods.

Young pets need special care. This kitten named Sasha is having her nails cut by a veterinarian.

Next, Sasha is weighed. The veterinarian keeps records of the kitten's weight, just as your doctor does for you. This helps her know if the kitten is healthy. Sasha also gets shots that will help keep her from getting sick.

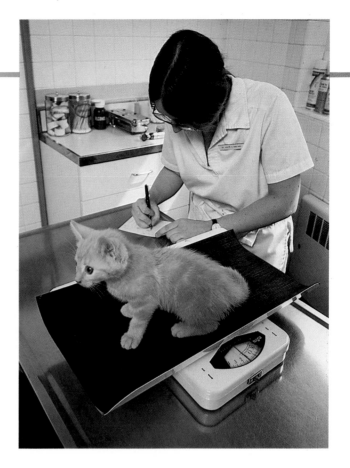

Using a special light, a veterinarian looks into the ear of a golden retriever. The assistant gently holds its mouth shut. Veterinarians say that you should bring your pets in for a checkup every year to help them stay well.

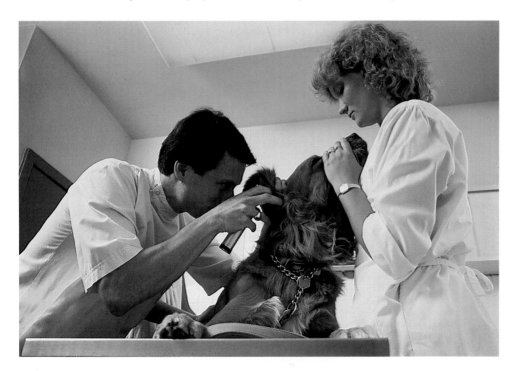

Pets need exercise to stay healthy and to keep from becoming bored. During a walk, dogs enjoy the sights and smells of the outdoors.

On a bright day, these children are taking their dogs for a walk along a river. They practice teaching the dogs to walk beside them. "Heel," they command.

If you have a dog, you can learn how to train it at a dog obedience class. A well-trained dog is a happier and safer pet. It is not as likely to run into danger if it stays by your side.

Time to play! Whitney pats his tabby cat and gives him catnip toys. The cat loves his toy mouse! He tosses it in the air and catches it, scratches it, and bites it.

Animals can be wonderful friends. Your pets need your help all their lives. How can you help them best? By being a good friend yourself!

On a rainy day, a wet little kitten gets a helping hand from a friend with an umbrella.
COVER: A girl gives her bearded collie a hug. Pets need love
and attention as well as food and shelter.

Published by The National Geographic Society, Washington, D.C.

Gilbert M. Grosvenor, *President*
Melvin M. Payne, *Chairman of the Board*
Owen R. Anderson, *Executive Vice President*
Robert L. Breeden, *Vice President, Publications and Educational Media*

Prepared by The Special Publications Division

Donald J. Crump, *Director*
Philip B. Silcott, *Associate Director*
William L. Allen, *Assistant Director*

Staff for this book

Jane H. Buxton, *Managing Editor*
David P. Johnson, *Picture Editor*
Turner Houston, *Art Director*
Gail N. Hawkins, *Researcher*
Carol Rocheleau Curtis, *Illustrations Assistant*
Elizabeth Ann Brazerol, Dianne T. Craven, Mary Elizabeth Davis, Rosamund Garner, Annie Hampford, Virginia W. Hannasch,
   Artemis S. Lampathakis, Cleo Petroff, Pamela Black Townsend, Virginia A. Williams, Eric Wilson, *Staff Assistants*

Engraving, Printing, and Product Manufacture

Robert W. Messer, *Manager*
George V. White, *Production Manager*
George J. Zeller, Jr., *Production Project Manager*
Mark R. Dunlevy, David V. Showers, Gregory Storer, *Assistant Production Managers;* Mary A. Bennett, *Production Assistant;*
   Julia F. Warner, *Production Staff Assistant*

Consultants

Lynda Bush, *Reading Consultant*
Karen O. Strimple, *Educational Consultant*
Guy R. Hodge, The Humane Society of the United States; Earl O. Strimple, D.V.M., *Scientific Consultants*

Illustrations Credits

All photographs by Susan McElhinney except: Steve Solum/BRUCE COLEMAN, INC. (10 upper); L. West/BRUCE COLEMAN, INC. (10
   lower); Julie Habel/WEST LIGHT (10-11, 22, 25, 32); Pat Lanza Field/BRUCE COLEMAN, INC. (13 upper); Keith Gunnar/BRUCE
   COLEMAN, INC. (20-21).

Library of Congress CIP Data

Rinard, Judith E.   Helping our animal friends.   (Books for young explorers)
     Summary: Children demonstrate proper care of pets and of sick or helpless wild animals that may need our help from time to time.
     1. Pets—Juvenile literature. 2. Animals—Juvenile literature. [1. Pets. 2. Animals] I. Title. II. Series.
SF416.2.R56   1985   636.08'87   85-2994
ISBN 0-87044-559-6 (regular edition)
ISBN 0-87044-564-2 (library edition)

For centuries, people of all ages have enjoyed keeping cats, dogs, birds, tropical fish, hamsters, and even snakes as pets. The animals provide companionship, amusement, and pleasure for their owners. But in return, pets need help from their owners in many ways.

Most pets need five things: good care, food, water, shelter, and love. Some animals need more attention than others do. When deciding what pet to choose, first consider the needs of the animal and whether you can fill them.

One consideration in choosing a pet is the size of your home and yard. Big animals need plenty of space for exercise (5-8).* Do you have time to take a large dog for walks every day (28-29)? It is wrong to keep an animal that needs exercise cooped up inside or tied up outside because it will become bored and frustrated.

Goldfish and other small pets such as birds need less care than dogs and cats do. Fish can be fed small amounts several times a day, and their water should be changed regularly. Keeping fishbowls and the cages of small animals clean (12-13) is very important in helping prevent diseases.

Birds that fly, such as parakeets and canaries, should have a cage large enough for them to fly about in. Birds should be let out of their cage for an hour or so daily in a room in which you have covered mirrors and windows and removed electrical appliances. Toys in the cage—a mirror, bell, ladder—add interest for the pet.

In feeding any pet, offer a properly balanced diet for the animal (9), not table scraps. Use clean feeding dishes

Birds	Feeders & Foods
American Goldfinch and Pine Siskin	Prefer hanging feeders. Canary seed, nutmeats, sunflower seeds, thistle seeds*
American Robin	Prefers ground feeders. Cheese, currants, any chopped fruits, raisins*
Bluebirds	Use most feeders. Cheese, chopped unsalted peanuts, currants, fine cracked corn, raisins, small berries,* suet
Chickadees and Titmice	Prefer hanging feeders. Canary seed, nutmeats, pumpkin seeds, suet, sunflower seeds,* raw peanuts*
House Finch	Uses most feeders. Canary seed, cut fruits, millet, nutmeats, suet, sunflower seeds,* thistle seeds
Hummingbirds	Use hummingbird feeders (wash frequently). Boiled sugar-water solution of one part sugar to four parts water
Jays: Blue, Scrub, and Steller's	Prefer ground feeders. Fine cracked corn, nutmeats, raisins, suet, sunflower seeds,* unshelled raw peanuts*
Northern Cardinal	Uses most feeders. Barley, fine cracked corn, millet, nutmeats, suet, sunflower seeds,* unsalted peanuts
Woodpeckers	Prefer tree-trunk feeders. Cheese, cut fruits, meat scraps, nutmeats, suet*

*Preferred foods

A variety of birds will visit your yard, no matter where you live, if you put up appetizing feeders. Birds, like people, have different tastes in foods. The chart above shows what foods some species like best. Place your feeders near tree branches, bushes, or other high cover so the birds can escape predators. As you watch your guests feeding, try to see which foods they eat most often. Observe how they use their beaks to eat. You may want to use binoculars for a closer view, and record your observations. You can feed birds in any season, but it is especially important in winter, when food is scarce. Soon, while giving them a helping hand, you will become an expert at identifying your bird neighbors.

*Numbers in parentheses refer to pages in *Helping Our Animal Friends.*

and keep plenty of water available at all times.

Veterinarians recommend that you bring in a new pet cat, dog, or bird—especially a young one—for a check-up as soon as possible. The veterinarian will examine the animal and look for parasites and signs of sickness. The veterinarian will also give a cat or dog vaccinations to protect it against diseases such as rabies and distemper.

As your pet grows, watch it for signs of illness or distress, such as vomiting, loss of appetite, shaking its head, or any unusual behavior. These signs tell you that your pet needs help and you should take it to a veterinarian.

Be sure your cat or dog wears an identification tag that gives your name, address, and telephone number. You should not let the animal run loose.

You can help a furry pet by grooming it. Long-haired animals need frequent brushing to stay healthy. A bath for a dog can help remove fleas and ticks that leave painful bites (17). Your veterinarian can recommend flea collars or sprays. Some birds should be sprayed weekly with mist to dampen their feathers.

Remember to protect your cat or dog during cold or hot weather. Never leave your pet outside on an extremely cold night. It might freeze to death. And in summer, never leave a pet in a car even for a few minutes. Even with the windows open, the car can become dangerously hot.

Playing with your pet can be a lot of fun as well as a good way of giving the animal the exercise it needs (30-31). Set aside a special time each day for play. Kittens and puppies love toys such as rubber balls and soft things to chew on. You can find a variety of good toys at a pet store or pet section of your supermarket. You may also want to try making a toy yourself.

To make a catnip mouse or round toy, buy a box of dried catnip at a pet store or supermarket. You'll need pieces of cotton material or felt. You may cut out either two mouse-shaped body pieces, or two simple circles. Sew the pieces together, with the outside facing in. Leave a small hole so you can turn the fabric right side out. If you make a mouse shape, cut out two small ears.

Next, turn the fabric right side out and stuff the catnip inside. Then sew up the hole. Sew or glue on the two felt ears for the mouse, and sew on a yarn or string tail. Draw on eyes with a marking pen. If you make a simple round toy, you can attach a string to it and tie on a small bell. Your kitten will love chasing it and pouncing at it.

Wild animals take care of themselves. But some may occasionally need help from people. In winter wild birds may have a hard time finding enough to eat. You can help them by putting up a bird feeder (10).

You can build a feeder yourself or buy one. Most libraries have information on how to construct a feeder. If you buy one, be sure it does not have sharp edges or gaps between connecting parts that can injure birds.

It is best to buy bird seed for your feeder at a feed and grain store or by mail order from a seed and grain catalog. Many birds also enjoy suet, a kind of fat you can buy from the butcher at your market.

Squirrels need extra food in winter too. So try building a squirrel feeder (10). Stock it with peanuts and other nuts, dried corn, and bits of apple.

Sometimes you may see a baby bird or squirrel or other young wild animal that looks helpless, but remember: Most young wild animals that seem to be in danger and abandoned by their parents really aren't! They may be learning to fly or to hunt for food with their parents nearby, but hidden. Be sure that the animal needs help before you do anything.

Adults, rather than children, should handle wild animals (22-23, 24-25). Remember that young animals are very fragile and require careful handling. Their first need is a warm, safe place to rest. Use a cardboard box filled with unscented tissue paper as a temporary nest. Keep the baby animal warm by placing a heating pad set on low or a hot water bottle wrapped with cloth on one side of the box. The animal should be able to move closer to or farther away from the heat.

Then get the baby animal to a wildlife specialist called a rehabilitator as soon as possible. These experts are trained and licensed to care for orphaned or injured wildlife and have the facilities to do so.

You can locate a rehabilitator by calling your local Humane Society, veterinarian, animal shelter, or nature center. When the animal is ready, the rehabilitator will return it to the wild.

You can help both wild and tame animals in a number of ways. Animals, in turn, help us by giving us beauty, enjoyment, and just by being a part of our world.

ADDITIONAL READING

Care of the Wild, Feathered and Furred, by Mae Hickman and Maxine Guy. (Santa Cruz, Unity Press, 1973). Family reference.

The Children's Book of Animals Around Us, ed. by Bridget Gibbs and Roz Kidman-Cox. (London, Usborne Ltd., 1978). Ages 8 and up.

The Well Cat Book and *The Well Dog Book,* by Terri McGinnis, D.V.M. (N.Y., Random House, 1975, 1974). Family reference.

Your World of Pets, by Susan McGrath. (Washington, D.C., National Geographic Society, 1985). Ages 8 and up.